W9-AHK-212

GERMANTOWN ELEMENTARY SCHOOL LIBRARY

Patterns

What Comes Next?

by Michele Koomen

Consultant:
Deborah S. Ermoian
Mathematics Faculty
Phoenix College
Phoenix, Arizona

Bridgestone Books
an imprint of Capstone Press
Mankato, Minnesota

Bridgestone Books are published by Capstone Press
151 Good Counsel Drive, P.O. Box 669, Mankato, Minnesota 56002
http://www.capstone-press.com

Copyright © 2001 Capstone Press. All rights reserved.
No part of this book may be reproduced without written permission from the publisher.
The publisher takes no responsibility for the use of any of the materials
or methods described in this book, nor for the products thereof.
Printed in the United States of America.

Library of Congress Cataloging-in-Publication Data
Koomen, Michele.
    Patterns: what comes next?/by Michele Koomen.
    p. cm.—(Exploring math)
    Includes bibliographical references and index.
    ISBN 0-7368-0819-1
    1. Sequences (Mathematics)—Juvenile literature. 2. Pattern perception—Juvenile
literature. [1. Pattern perception. 2. Sequences (Mathematics)] I. Title. II. Series.
QA292 .K66 2001
515'.24—dc21   00-010561

Summary: Simple text, photographs, and illustrations introduce mathematical patterns,
    including how to identify patterns, create patterns, and predict what comes next in
    a given pattern.

Editorial Credits
Tom Adamson, editor; Lois Wallentine, product planning editor; Linda Clavel, designer;
    Katy Kudela, photo researcher

Photo Credits
Artville/Jeff Burke and Lorraine Triolo, 4
Capstone Press, cover
Capstone Press/CG Book Printers, 8–9
Gregg Andersen, 17, 20 (top), 21 (bottom)
Image Farm Inc., 20 (bottom)
Kimberly Danger, 6
Root Resources/Ruth Cordner, 21 (top)

1 2 3 4 5 6 06 05 04 03 02 01

Table of Contents

What Is a Pattern?

A pattern is the placement of objects in some kind of order. These apples show a pattern. They are placed in a certain way. A red apple comes first. A green one comes next. The color pattern repeats.

A B A B A B

Patterns of Position

These kids are showing a pattern of position. The pattern is standing, sitting, standing, sitting. You can use letters to represent the pattern. The letter "A" is for standing. The letter "B" is for sitting. The pattern is ABABAB.

Patterns of Size

These balls show a pattern of size. Size is how large or small something is. The pattern is large ball, large ball, small ball, small ball. The pattern repeats.

A   A   B   B

You can use letters to represent the pattern. The letter "A" stands for large ball. The letter "B" stands for small ball. The pattern is AABBAABB.

A   A   B   B

?

Patterns of Color

These crayons show a pattern of color. The pattern is red, green, blue, red, green, blue. The pattern is ABCABC. What color does each letter represent? What color should come next in the pattern?

Checkerboard Pattern

This game board shows a checkerboard pattern. First there is a white square, then a black square, then a white square, and so on. The same pattern goes across and down the whole board.

A
A
A
B
A
A
A
B
A
A
B

Growing Patterns

This string of beads shows a growing pattern. First there is 1 green bead, then 1 blue bead. Next, 2 green beads are added and then 1 blue bead. An extra green bead is added each time the pattern repeats.

The growing pattern begins with the letters ABAABAAAB. What letters come next in the pattern?

Skip Counting by 2s

You can use skip counting to count objects quickly. Skip every other number when you skip count by 2s. You make a number pattern when you skip count.

Count these socks 2 at a time.
The number pattern is 2, 4, 6, 8.
There are 8 socks.

2

4

6

8

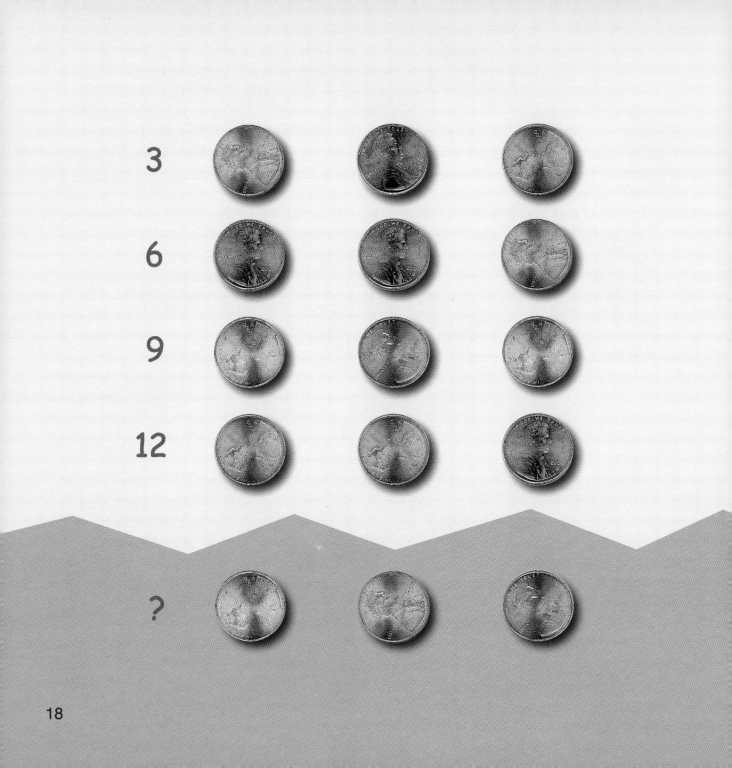

3

6

9

12

?

Skip Counting by 3s

There are 3 pennies in each row. You can skip count by 3s to find the number of pennies. The number pattern is 3, 6, 9, 12. There are 12 pennies in the picture. How many pennies are there when one row of pennies is added? What if two more rows were added?

Patterns Are All around Us

You can see patterns
in your neighborhood.

This fence shows
a pattern. ▶

◀ This road sign also
shows a pattern.

You also can
see patterns on
animals. This
ring-tailed
lemur has a
color pattern
on its tail.

This fish
also has a
color pattern.
Patterns repeat
their designs.

Hands On: Making Patterns

A pattern shows some kind of order. You can make your own patterns with everyday objects.

What You Need

Two people
A variety of small objects:

Buttons	Crayons
Old keys	Coins
Stickers	

Or make shapes with paper

What You Do

1. One person builds a pattern using some of the objects. For example, the pattern could be ABABAB.
2. The second person copies that pattern using different objects.
3. Use different objects to make other patterns such as AABBAABB, ABCABC, ABBABBABB.
4. Make more patterns. Take turns making the first pattern. Make as many types of patterns as you can.
5. Have one person invent a pattern using any of the objects. The other person tries to figure out what comes next in the pattern using the objects. When you find the pattern, you can say what objects come next in the pattern.

Words to Know

design (di-ZINE)—the shape or style of something

growing pattern (GROH-wing PAT-urn)—a pattern that adds an item each time the pattern repeats

pattern (PAT-urn)—a repeating arrangement of colors, shapes, or objects

position (puh-ZISH-uhn)—the way in which someone is standing, sitting, or lying

represent (rep-ri-ZENT)—to stand for something

Read More

Bryant-Mole, Karen. *Patterns*. Mortimer's Math. Milwaukee: Gareth Stevens, 2000.

Murphy, Stuart J. *Beep Beep, Vroom Vroom!* MathStart. New York: HarperCollins, 2000.

Patilla, Peter. *Patterns*. Math Links. Des Plaines, Ill.: Heinemann Library, 1999.

Reid, Margarette S. *A String of Beads*. New York: Dutton Children's Books. 1997.

Internet Sites

Ask Dr. Math
http://mathforum.com/dr.math
Figure This! Math Challenges for Families
http://www.figurethis.org
MathSteps
http://www.eduplace.com/math/mathsteps/index.html

Index